Cowboy
Coloring Book For Kids!

A Variety
Of Unique
Cowboy
Coloring Pages
For Children

No part of this book may be reproduced or used in any way or form or by any means whether electronic or mechanical, this means that you cannot record or photocopy any material ideas or tips that are provided in this book.

Copyright 2021

This is a Bleed-through page if you are using a coloring marker or pen!

Bold Illustrations

This is a Bleed-through page if you are using a coloring marker or pen!

Bold Illustrations

This is a Bleed-through page if you are using a coloring marker or pen!

Bold Illustrations

This is a Bleed-through page if you are using a coloring marker or pen!

Bold Illustrations

This is a Bleed-through page if you are using a coloring marker or pen!

Bold Illustrations

This is a Bleed-through page if you are using a coloring marker or pen!

Bold Illustrations

This is a Bleed-through page if you are using a coloring marker or pen!

Bold Illustrations

This is a Bleed-through page if you are using a coloring marker or pen!

Bold Illustrations

This is a Bleed-through page if you are using a coloring marker or pen!

Bold Illustrations

This is a Bleed-through page if you are using a coloring marker or pen!

Bold Illustrations

This is a Bleed-through page if you are using a coloring marker or pen!

Bold Illustrations

This is a Bleed-through page if you are using a coloring marker or pen!

Bold Illustrations

This is a Bleed-through page if you are using a coloring marker or pen!

Bold Illustrations

This is a Bleed-through page if you are using a coloring marker or pen!

Bold Illustrations

This is a Bleed-through page if you are using a coloring marker or pen!

Bold Illustrations

This is a Bleed-through page if you are using a coloring marker or pen!

Bold Illustrations

This is a Bleed-through page if you are using a coloring marker or pen!

Bold Illustrations

This is a Bleed-through page if you are using a coloring marker or pen!

Bold Illustrations

This is a Bleed-through page if you are using a coloring marker or pen!

Bold Illustrations

This is a Bleed-through page if you are using a coloring marker or pen!

Bold Illustrations

This is a Bleed-through page if you are using a coloring marker or pen!

Bold Illustrations

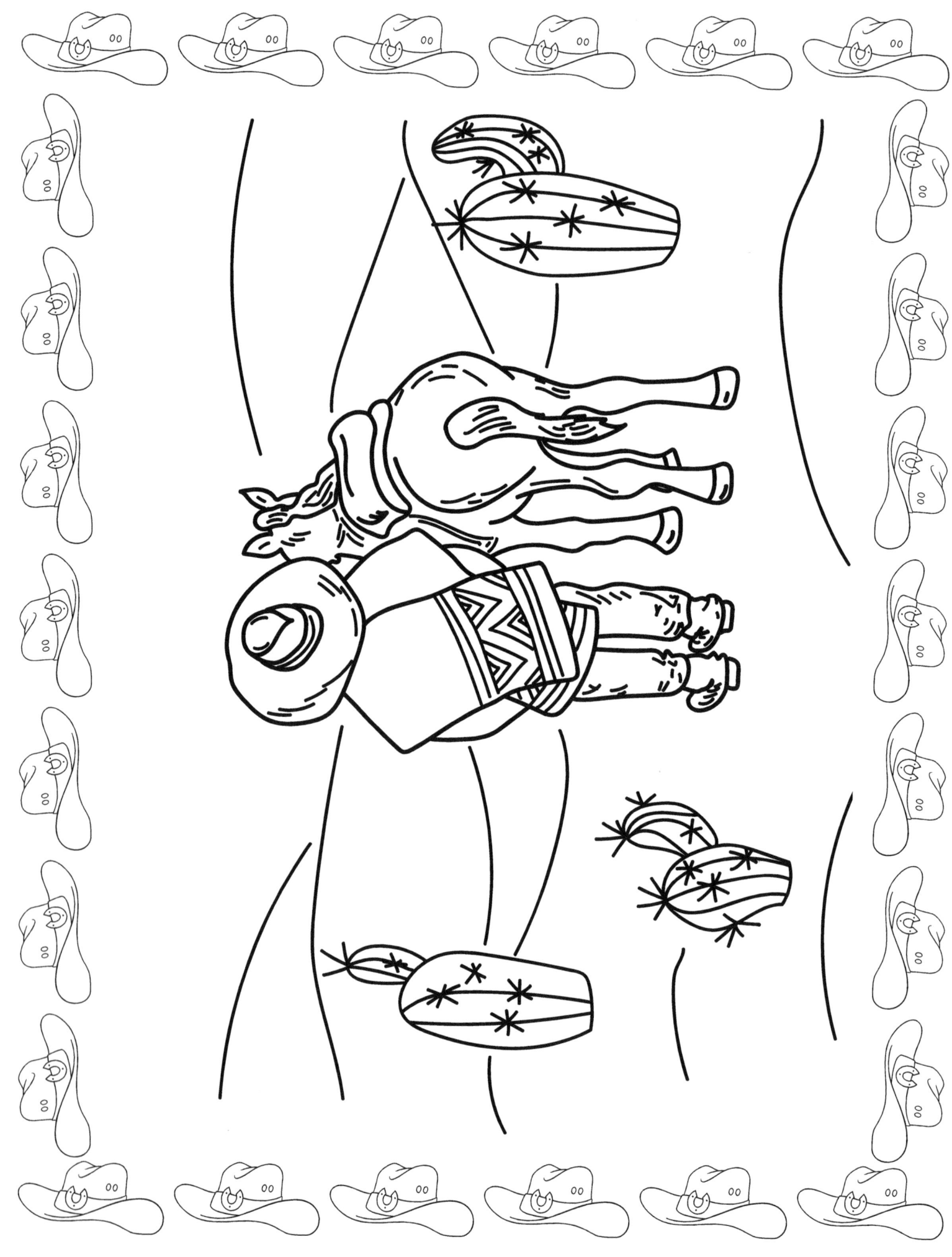

This is a Bleed-through page if you are using a coloring marker or pen!

Bold Illustrations

This is a Bleed-through page if you are using a coloring marker or pen!

Bold Illustrations

This is a Bleed-through page if you are using a coloring marker or pen!

Bold Illustrations

This is a Bleed-through page if you are using a coloring marker or pen!

Bold Illustrations

This is a Bleed-through page if you are using a coloring marker or pen!

Bold Illustrations

This is a Bleed-through page if you are using a coloring marker or pen!

Bold Illustrations

This is a Bleed-through page if you are using a coloring marker or pen!

Bold Illustrations

This is a Bleed-through page if you are using a coloring marker or pen!

Bold Illustrations

This is a Bleed-through page if you are using a coloring marker or pen!

Bold Illustrations

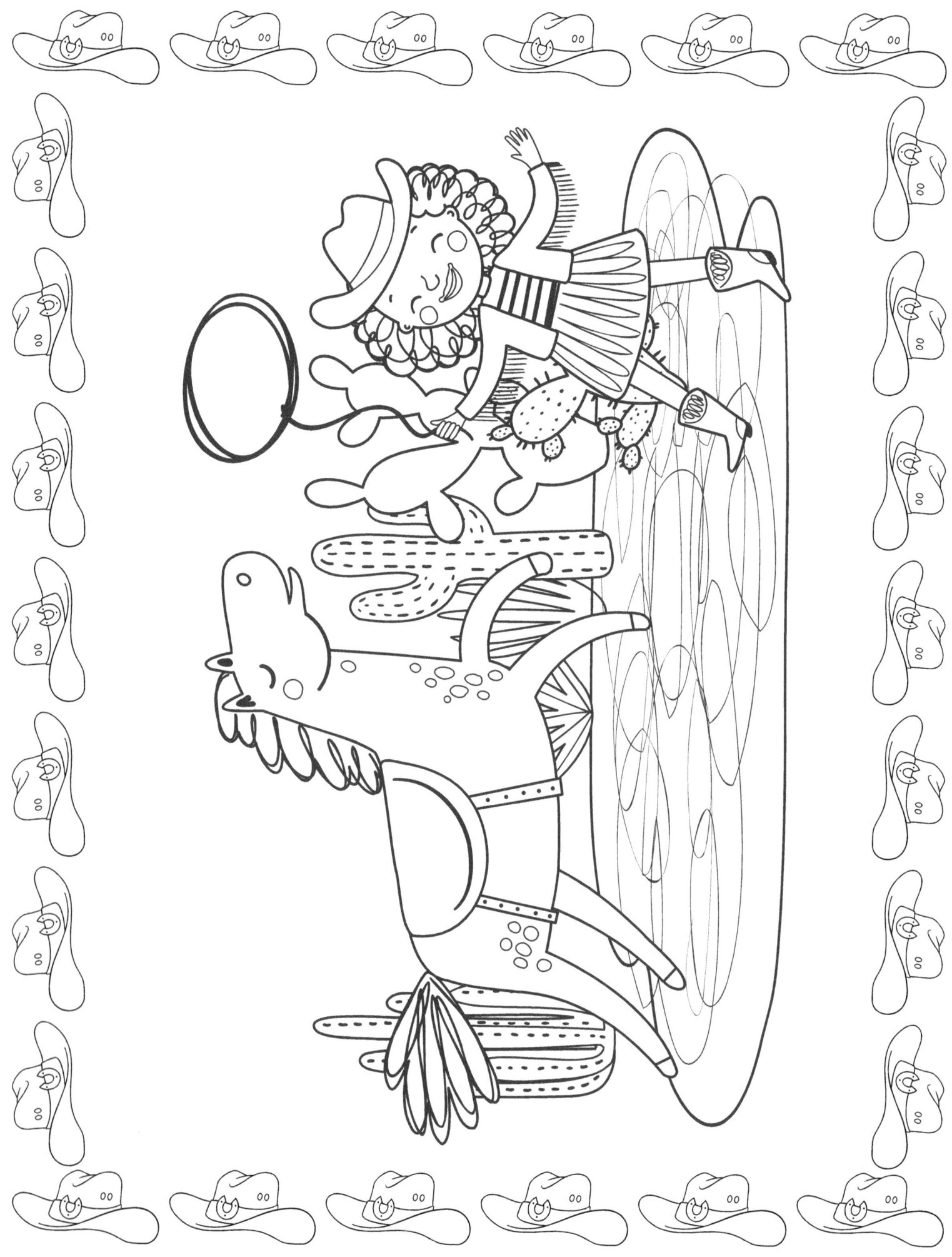

This is a Bleed-through page if you are using a coloring marker or pen!

Bold Illustrations

This is a Bleed-through page if you are using a coloring marker or pen!

Bold Illustrations

This is a Bleed-through page if you are using a coloring marker or pen!

Bold Illustrations

This is a Bleed-through page if you are using a coloring marker or pen!

Bold Illustrations

This is a Bleed-through page if you are using a coloring marker or pen!

Bold Illustrations

This is a Bleed-through page if you are using a coloring marker or pen!

Bold Illustrations

This is a Bleed-through page if you are using a coloring marker or pen!

Bold Illustrations

This is a Bleed-through page if you are using a coloring marker or pen!

Bold Illustrations

This is a Bleed-through page if you are using a coloring marker or pen!

Bold Illustrations

This is a Bleed-through page if you are using a coloring marker or pen!

Bold Illustrations

Lightning Source UK Ltd.
Milton Keynes UK
UKHW030432100922
408624UK00003B/90